PRAYER AT NIGHT
A Book for the Darkness

❖❖❖❖❖❖❖❖❖❖❖❖❖❖❖❖❖❖❖❖❖❖❖❖❖

JIM COTTER

SHEFFIELD
CAIRNS PUBLICATIONS
1991

First published 1983
Fourth edition 1988
Reprinted with minor amendments 1991
Reprinted 1994

The illustration *Encounter* is by M. C. Escher
© Copyright by Escher Heirs, and used by permission

This book is also available in standard size
Copies may be obtained from
Cairns Publications
47 Firth Park Avenue, Sheffield S5 6HF

Companion volumes, also in both standard and pocket sizes
Prayer in the Morning
Prayer in the Day

Printed by J.W. Northend Ltd
Clyde Road, Sheffield S8 0TZ

SEQUENCE

WITH GRATITUDE TO THOSE
*who have helped me take a few steps
in the way of God's Love,
and in particular to those
who have encouraged and assisted me
in the compiling of* Prayer at Night:

JANE of Fairacres

NADIR of Jersey

ESTHER of Canterbury

RYDER of London

PREFACE

THE reprinting of the fourth edition of *Prayer at Night*, in both pocket and standard size, gives me the opportunity of revising the Preface. Since it was first published ten years ago, the book has sold twelve thousand copies, and I have been moved by the letters of appreciation sent to me. I should like the acknowledgment on the opposite page to include those unnamed correspondents as well as the named friends who first encouraged me.

The book came to be written in this way. I had been praying Compline in a modern English version. It occurred to me that I had addressed God as 'Lord' rather frequently in no more than ten minutes. In fact it was thirty-six times. 'Father' came second with twelve. All the other biblical images of God were either omitted or rarely used.

At the time I was beginning to realize that the prayer of the Christian Church had been slanted by a patriarchy and hierarchy of men who took nearly all the decisions and held nearly all the power. Rather than merely criticize, I thought I had better attempt a variant. So *Prayer at Night* was born, with its intention of using a greater variety of both picture language and overall material than does the traditional order, yet keeping the same structure.

Some find the more official modern language versions of Compline simple and austere, others find them repetitive and threadbare. For the latter, *Prayer at Night* seems to have struck a chord and enabled them to keep on praying. One correspondent wrote that she could use the book at the end of a heavy day when her brain was hurting.

Companion volumes have followed, *Prayer in the Day* and *Prayer in the Morning*, both in print, and offering words that can be prayed through without rush and within a quarter of an hour, each echoing the traditional 'offices' of the Church, but usable at home or on the bus. I hope that *Prayer at Night* will be found helpful both at the end of the day and during the night, in hours of sleeplessness or vigil.

If the service is used corporately, it may be found appropriate for the whole company to say those parts which have a vertical line by them in the margin – though in saying the Psalms in small groups, each person in turn could say a couple of lines.

The second part of the compilation, "That Day and Night shall be a single whole", is a sequence of meditations to set alongside the more formal first part. They are offered as "Cairns for a journey" through dark places – not a detailed map, but markers on a trail that one person has found useful. Some are quotations or adaptations: these are indented on the page. The rest often echo the words of others. I have acknowledged these in the notes at the end of the book, and I hope I may be forgiven any omissions owing to bad memory. In many of the thoughts, the 'speaker' addressing the 'reader' may be a kind of guardian angel.

I am grateful to Mother (now Sister) Jane for the Foreword. The title of the second part comes from her observation that in praying in the early hours of the morning the Sisters of the Love of God are aiming to make of the 'night' and 'day' a single whole Day of twenty-four hours. Too often do we exclude, repress, and project the 'dark', to the world's great danger and our own withering.

That *A New Zealand Prayer Book* should have incorporated substantial parts of *Prayer at Night* brings vividly alive the thought that indeed the twenty-four hours are being prayed through as light and darkness move round our planet.

Finally, I want to express my thanks to Alan Dodson of Malvern, typographer, for his professional advice on the layout of this book, and for his design of the cover.

JIM COTTER, *January* 1991

FOREWORD

THE Office of Compline is sometimes referred to as 'the goodnight prayer of the Church', with the implication that it is a sort of liturgical lullaby rounding off the day and designed to ensure a quiet night. This can be justified, as in the paraphrase of the psalm in these pages: "I lie down in peace, and sleep comes at once, for in you alone, O God, do I dwell unafraid."

But praying at night involves considerably more than a peaceful passage through the hours of darkness. We 'let go' into sleep just as, one day, we shall have to 'let go' into death; and it is good to get accustomed to something of what this surrender involves. One of the final prayers for daily use in *Prayer at Night* says this beautifully,

> "O living God, in Jesus Christ you were laid in the tomb at this evening hour, and so sanctified the grave to be a bed of hope to your people. Grant us courage and faith to die daily to our sin and pride, that even as this flesh and blood decays, our lives still may grow in you, that at our last day our dying may be done so well that we live in you for ever."

The night hours are concerned with conflict as well as quietness, and so preparation for them includes claiming the armour of God for spiritual struggle and filling our minds with a range of strong biblical imagery in order to make a positive affirmation that God is Love. We also need to be ready to explore what this statement means in itself and what it demands from us – an exercise which will not necessarily lead to comfort or reassurance.

Prayer in the night is different from prayer in the day. Whether it is 'waiting for the dawn' in the early hours, or 'doing battle' with the 'powers of evil' in the middle of the night, it requires a naked exposure before God – the kind of nakedness that can be clothed in the daytime by those familiar distractions which make it more difficult to stay still and keep attentive to God. So a liturgical office which is a gateway into the night needs to take account of this fact. Here we are given a form of Compline which is as sharp as well as consoling in its reality and relevance. It stands on its own, but could equally well fit into the daily cycle of the parochial or monastic office. It is based on the traditional pattern of: Introduction, Confession, Psalmody, Reading, Hymn, Nunc Dimittis, Prayer(s), and Blessing. In each main section there is provision for a weekly/monthly cycle, and for special feasts and occasions. There is a full and varied collection of prayers and meditations at the end. The whole has undoubtedly emerged from the prayed experience of the compiler, and so evokes a similar response in the user.

For example, the confessions – different for each day of the week – taken together do not let us get away with the meaningless mutter that can, in a familiar formula, all too easily pass for penitence. Because on Friday and Saturday we spell out our nastiness and face its effect on other people, and we see just how our personal indifference and careless-ness react negatively within the whole of creation, the more traditional phraseology of previous evenings comes alive, and the words have their intended impact. The choice of psalms, and the subtleties of the paraphrasing, both encourage and challenge us. There is a lot here about light piercing dark-ness, about mercy and forgiveness, about trust in God: above all, there is praise, worship, awe, in face of the 'Creator of the ever-changing hills'. God is our refuge and strength, and gives us gifts even while we sleep, but also the inescapable, all-knowing fashioner of 'cell and tissue, blood and bone' who searches us out and holds us, as in the palm of a hand.

Prayer at Night is authentic because in it the wisdom of the centuries, in scripture and above all in the psalms, is filled out by contemporary Christian experience of God as 'Life-giver,

Pain-bearer, Love-maker' – a phrase that makes us think what
we mean when we use the familiar trinitarian formula – and
the awareness that each of us who tries to pray is part of the
human whole, subject to all manner of powers of darkness,
including of course the ever-present threat of nuclear extinc-
tion. So we are taken over the threshold from daytime, not
in a holy huddle of 'me, myself, and God', but, whether
prayed alone or in company, as representatives of humanity,
acknowledging creaturehood before God – but also humbly
grateful for our partnership with God in that loving work of
redemption which 'pours out lifeblood in love for us', and
indeed asks the same of us.

JANE, SLG

Encounter by M. C. Escher

PRAYERS
of Introduction and of Recognition
and
PSALMS

SUNDAY

THE ANGELS of God guard us through the night,
| and quieten the powers of darkness.
The Spirit of God be our guide
| to lead us to peace and to glory.

People of God, be sober, be watchful: your adversary the devil as a roaring lion prowls about, seeking someone to devour; whom withstand, steadfast in the faith.

Our help is in the name of the eternal God,
| who is making the heavens and the earth.

DEAR GOD, thank you for all that is good,
for our creation and our humanity,
for the stewardship you have given us of this planet
    earth,
for the gifts of life and of one another,
for your Love which is unbounded and eternal . . .

O Thou, Most Holy and Beloved,
my Companion, my Unicorn, my Guide upon the Way.

WE have wounded your love:
| O God, heal us.
We stumble in the darkness:
| Light of the world, transfigure us.
We forget that we are your home:
| Spirit of God, dwell in us.

O God of Joy, we rejoice in you . . .
You run to meet us like a welcoming friend,
you laugh with us in the merriment of heaven,
you feast with us at the great banquet,

Clown of clowns, Fool of fools,
the only Entertainer of Jesters.
O God of Joy, we rejoice in you . . .

ETERNAL SPIRIT, flow through our being and open our
    lips
| that our mouths may proclaim your praise.
    Let us worship the God of Love:
| Alleluia. Alleluia.

| FROM the deep places of my soul I praise you O God:
I lift up my heart and glorify your holy name.
From the deep places of my soul I praise you O God:
how can I forget all your goodness towards me?
You forgive all my sin, you heal all my weakness,
you rescue me from the brink of disaster,
you crown me with mercy and compassion.
You satisfy my being with good things,
so that my youth is renewed like an eagle's.
You fulfil all that you promise,
justice for all the oppressed.
You made known your ways to Moses,
and all the people saw your deeds.
You are full of forgiveness and grace,
endlessly patient, faithful in love.
You do not haunt us with our sins,
nor nurse grievances against us.
You do not repay evil with evil,
for you are greater than our sins.
As vast as the heavens are in comparison with the earth,
so great is your love to those who trust you.
As far as the east is from the west,
so far do you fling our sins from us.
Just as parents are merciful to their children,
so are you merciful and kind towards us.

For you know how fragile we are,
that we are made of the dust of the earth.
Our days are like the grass,
they bloom like the flowers of the field:
the wind blows over them and they are gone,
and no-one can tell where they stood.
Only your merciful goodness endures;
age after age you act justly
towards all who hold on to your covenant,
who take your words to heart and fulfil them.

For you have triumphed over the power of death,
and draw us to your presence with songs of joy.
We hear the echo of your angels praising you,
and the whole communion of your saints,
those who have walked in your narrow ways,
and heard the voice of your yearning,
whose food is to do your will,
and in whom you take great delight.
From the widest bounds of the universe
to the depths of my very being,
the whispers and cries of joy
vibrate to a shining glory,
O God, our beginning and our end.

MONDAY

THE ANGELS of God guard us through the night,
 | and quieten the powers of darkness.
The Spirit of God be our guide
 | to lead us to peace and to glory.

They that wait for the Spirit shall renew their strength: they shall mount up with wings as eagles, they shall run and not be weary, they shall walk and not faint.

Our help is in the name of the eternal God,
 | who is making the heavens and the earth.

DEAR GOD, thank you for all that is good,
for our creation and our humanity,
for the stewardship you have given us of this planet
    earth,
for the gifts of life and of one another,
for your Love which is unbounded and eternal . . .

O Thou, Most Holy and Beloved,
my Companion, my Unicorn, my Guide upon the Way.

WE grieve and confess
that we hurt and have been hurt,
to the third and fourth generations,
that we are so afraid of pain
that we shield ourselves from being vulnerable to
    others,
and refuse to be open and trusting as a child . . .

O God of Wholeness, we rest in you . . .
You listen with us to the sound of running water,
you sit with us under the shade of the trees of our
    healing,
you walk once more with us in the garden in the cool of
    the day,
the oil of your anointing penetrates the cells of our
    being,
the warmth of your hands steadies us and gives us
    courage.
O God of Wholeness, we rest in you . . .

ETERNAL SPIRIT, flow through our being and open our
    lips
| that our mouths may proclaim your praise.
Let us worship the God of Love:
| Alleluia. Alleluia.

WE your servants bless you, O God,
as we stand by night in your house.
We lift up our hands towards the holy place,
and give you thanks and praise.
Bless us from all places where you dwell,
O God, Creator of the heavens and the earth.

ANSWER me when I call, O God,
for you are the God of Justice.
You set me free when I was hard-pressed:
be gracious to me now and hear my prayer.
Men and women, how long will you turn my glory to
    my shame?
How long will you love what is worthless and run after
    lies?

Know that God has shown me such wonderful kindness;
when I call out in prayer, God hears me.
Tremble, admit defeat, and sin no more.
Look deep into your heart before you sleep and be still.
Bring your gifts, just as you are,
and put your trust in God.
Many are asking, Who can make us content?
The light of your countenance has gone from us,
    O God.
Yet you have given my heart more gladness
than those whose corn and wine and oil increase.
I lie down in peace and sleep comes at once,
for in you alone, O God, do I dwell unafraid.

DEAR GOD, you sustain me and feed me:
like a shepherd you guide me.
You lead me to an oasis of green,
to lie down by restful waters.
You refresh my soul for the journey,
and guide me along trusted roads.
The God of Justice is your name.
Though I must enter the darkness of death,
I will fear no evil.
For you are with me,
your rod and your staff comfort me.
You prepare a table before my very eyes,
in the presence of those who trouble me.
You anoint my head with oil,
and you fill my cup to the brim.
Your loving kindness and mercy will meet me every day
    of my life,
and I will dwell in the house of my God for ever.

TUESDAY

THE ANGELS of God guard us through the night,
| and quieten the powers of darkness.
The Spirit of God be our guide
| to lead us to peace and to glory.

God is spirit and those who worship God must worship in
spirit and in truth.

Our help is in the name of the eternal God,
| who is making the heavens and the earth.

DEAR GOD, thank you for all that is good,
for our creation and our humanity,
for the stewardship you have given us of this planet
    earth,
for the gifts of life and of one another,
for your Love which is unbounded and eternal . . .

O Thou, Most Holy and Beloved,
my Companion, my Unicorn, my Guide upon the Way.

MERCIFUL GOD,
we have not loved you with our whole heart,
nor our neighbours as ourselves.
Forgive what we have been,
accept us as we are,
and guide what we shall be . . .

O God of Mercy, we thank you . . .
you forgive our past sin,
you strengthen us in your gift of eternal life,
you shape us for glory.
O God of Mercy, we thank you . . .

ETERNAL SPIRIT, flow through our being and open our
  lips
| that our mouths may proclaim your praise.
  Let us worship the God of Love:
| Alleluia. Alleluia.

I WILL lift up my eyes to the mountains,
but where shall I find help?
From you alone, O God, does my help come,
Creator of the ever-changing hills.
You will not let me stumble on the rough pathways,
you care for me and watch over me without ceasing.
I am sure that the Guardian of Israel neither slumbers
    nor sleeps.
The God of all peoples keeps watch,
like a shadow spread over me.
So the sun will not strike me by day,
nor the moon by night.
You will defend me in the presence of evil,
you will guard my life.
You will defend my going out and my coming in,
this night and always.

O GOD, I give you thanks for the wisdom of your
    counsel,
even at night you have instructed my heart.
I have set your face always before me,
you are at my right hand and I shall not fall.
Therefore my heart is glad and my spirit rejoices,
my flesh also shall rest secure.
For you will not give me over to the power of Death,
nor let your faithful one see the Pit.
In your presence is the fulness of joy,
and from your right hand flow delights for evermore.

O God, I have come to you for shelter:
let me never be put to shame.
Deliver me in the justice of your ways:
incline your ear to me and be swift to save me.
Be for me a rock of refuge, a fortress to defend me:
for you are my rock and my stronghold.
Lead me and guide me for your name's sake:
deliver me out of the net that they have laid secretly for
   me,
for you are my strength.
Into your hands I commit my spirit,
for you will redeem me, eternal God of Truth.

WEDNESDAY

THE ANGELS of God guard us through the night,
| and quieten the powers of darkness.
The Spirit of God be our guide
| to lead us to peace and to glory.

Be alert; stand firm in the faith; be valiant and strong. Let
everything you do be done in love.

Our help is in the name of the eternal God,
| who is making the heavens and the earth.

DEAR GOD, thank you for all that is good,
for our creation and our humanity,
for the stewardship you have given us of this planet
    earth,
for the gifts of life and of one another,
for your Love which is unbounded and eternal . . .

O Thou, Most Holy and Beloved,
my Companion, my Unicorn, my Guide upon the Way.

HEAR the wisdom of Jesus:
Abide in my love:
| Kyrie eleison.
Love your enemies:
| Christe eleison.
Love your neighbour as yourself:
| Kyrie eleison.
Love one another as I have loved you:
| Christe eleison.
Above all, love God with the whole of your being:
| Kyrie eleison.

O God of Forgiveness, we contemplate you . . .
You pour out your lifeblood in love for us,
you pursue us and disturb us and accept us,
you meet our sin and pain with the gift of a costly and
    infinite enduring, overcoming evil with good.
O God of Forgiveness, we contemplate you . . .

ETERNAL SPIRIT, flow through our being and open our
    lips
| that our mouths may proclaim your praise.
Let us worship the God of Love:
| Alleluia. Alleluia.

LIGHT OF LIGHT, you have searched me out and known
    me.
You know where I am and where I go,
you see my thoughts from afar.
You discern my paths and my resting places,
you are acquainted with all my ways.
Yes, and not a word comes from my lips
but you, O God, have heard it already.
You are in front of me and you are behind me,
you have laid your hand on my shoulder.
Such knowledge is too wonderful for me,
so great that I cannot fathom it.
Where shall I go from your Spirit,
where shall I flee from your Presence?
If I climb to the heavens you are there:
if I descend to the depths of the earth, you are there
    also.
If I spread my wings towards the morning,
and fly to the uttermost shores of the sea,
even there your hand will lead me,
and your right hand will hold me.

If I should cry to the darkness to cover me,
and the night to enclose me,
the darkness is no darkness to you,
and the night is as clear as the day.
For you have created every part of my being,
cell and tissue, blood and bone.
You have woven me in the womb of my mother;
I will praise you, so wonderfully am I made.
Awesome are your deeds and marvellous are your works.
You know me to the very core of my being;
nothing in me was hidden from your eyes
when I was formed in silence and secrecy,
in intricate splendour in the depths of the earth.
Even as they were forming you saw my limbs,
each part of my body shaped by your finger.
How deep are your thoughts to me, O God,
how great is the sum of them.
Were I to count them they are more in number
than the grains of sand upon the sea-shore –
and still I would know nothing about you –
yet still would you hold me in the palm of your hand.

THURSDAY

THE ANGELS of God guard us through the night,
| and quieten the powers of darkness.
The Spirit of God be our guide
| to lead us to peace and to glory.

Pray in the power of the Spirit. Keep watch and persevere, and remember all God's people.

Our help is in the name of the eternal God
| who is making the heavens and the earth.

DEAR GOD, thank you for all that is good,
for our creation and our humanity,
for the stewardship you have given us of this planet
    earth,
for the gifts of life and of one another,
for your Love which is unbounded and eternal . . .

O Thou, Most Holy and Beloved,
my Companion, my Unicorn, my Guide upon the Way.

LOVING GOD, close your eyes to our sins,
| we who have wounded your love.
Refine us with the flame of your Spirit:
| cleanse us with springs of living water.
Save us with words of forgiveness and peace:
| make us whole, steadfast in spirit.
Broken are our bones, yet you can heal us,
| and we shall leap for joy and dance again.

O God of Love, we adore you . . .
You transfigure our disfigured faces,
you strive with our resistant clay,
you bring out of our chaos, harmony.
O God of Love, we adore you . . .

ETERNAL SPIRIT, flow through our being and open our
   lips,
| that our mouths may proclaim your praise.
Let us worship the God of Love:
| Alleluia. Alleluia.

GOD IS our refuge and strength,
a very present help in time of trouble.
Therefore we shall not be afraid,
even though the earth be moved,
even though the mountains should crumble and fall
   into the sea,
even though the waters should foam and rage,
assault the cliffs and make them shudder.
   You are for us the God of the powers,
   a safe stronghold, the God of all peoples.

There is a river whose streams make glad the city of
   God.
Here is God's dwelling place and it will stand firm.
God's rescue dawns like the morning light,
God's voice echoes through every land.
When powerful nations panic and totter,
and the whole world comes crashing down,
   You are for us the God of the powers,
   a safe stronghold, the God of all peoples.

Come and see, stand in awe
at the powerful things God will do on the earth,
| putting an end to all war in the world,

breaking the bow, shattering the spear into splinters,
throwing our weapons on the fire.
"Be still and know that I am God:
exalted among the nations,
my name known at last on the earth."
    You are for us the God of the powers,
    a safe stronghold, the God of all peoples.

THEY who dwell in the shelter of the Most High,
who abide under the shadow of the Almighty,
say to our God,
You are my refuge and stronghold,
my God in whom I put my trust.
You set me free from the snare of the hunter,
and from evil's destroying curse.
You cover me with your wings,
and I shall be safe under your feathers.
Your faithfulness shall be my shield and defence.
In the dead of night I have no terror to fear,
neither dread in the daytime the plunge of the dagger,
nor fear the plague that stalks in the darkness,
nor the fever that strikes in the heat of the day.
For you, O God, will command your angels
to keep me in your narrow ways;
they will bear me up in their hands,
lest I dash my foot against a stone.
"Because I am bound to you in love,
therefore I will deliver you.
I will lift you out of danger
because you hold on to my name.
In your anguish and need I am with you,
I will set you free and clothe you with glory.
You will live to be full of years,
and you will know the abundance of my salvation."

FRIDAY

THE ANGELS of God guard us through the night,
| and quieten the powers of darkness.
The Spirit of God be our guide
| to lead us to peace and to glory.

Jesus said to his disciples, Were you not able to stay awake
for one hour? Keep watch, all of you, and pray that you will
not fail in time of testing.

Our help is in the name of the eternal God
| who is making the heavens and the earth.

DEAR GOD, thank you for all that is good,
for our creation and our humanity,
for the stewardship you have given us of this planet
    earth,
for the gifts of life and of one another,
for your Love which is unbounded and eternal . . .

O Thou, Most Holy and Beloved,
my Companion, my Unicorn, my Guide upon the Way.

WE confess our unfaithfulness:
| our pride, hypocrisy, and impatience;
our self-indulgent appetites and ways;
our exploitation of other people;
the violence, envy, and ruthless greed in our hearts and
    deeds;
our idleness in ease and comfort, and our possessiveness;
| our neglect of prayer, and our failure to live our faith.

O God of Holiness, we tremble in your presence . . .
You show us how far we have wandered in a land that
   is waste;
you face us with the truth of our lack of love;
you uncover the layers of our illusions;
you pierce us with the sword that heals;
you embrace us with a purging fire;
you refuse to let us go.
O God of Holiness, we tremble in your presence . . .

ETERNAL SPIRIT, flow through our being and open our
   lips
| that our mouths may proclaim your praise.
Let us worship the God of Love:
| Alleluia. Alleluia.

| OUT of the depths I have called to you, O God:
O God of compassion, hear my voice.
Open your heart to me, my cry wells within me.
If you keep account of my sins, I cannot stand.
But there is forgiveness with you, your way is my life.
I wait for you, my God, my soul waits for you.
I wait with my heart, I hope for your word.
I look for you as a watchman looks for the morning,
more I say than a watchman for the morning.
For you will fulfil your promise to rescue me,
you will free me from the grip of evil.
I put my trust in you,
| O God of mercy and compassion.

| WHEN God takes us home from our exile,
we shall wake from our dream and live again.
We shall sing and laugh for joy;
| the whole world will acclaim God's wonders.

O God, you will do great things for us,
and we shall rejoice and praise your name.
Take us home, bring us to life,
like rivers in the desert when the first rains fall.
We go on our way sadly,
with tears sowing seeds.
We shall return with joy,
with gladness bearing our sheaves.

SATURDAY

THE ANGELS of God guard us through the night
| and quieten the powers of darkness.
The Spirit of God be our guide
| to lead us to peace and to glory.

It is but lost labour that you haste to rise up early, and so late take rest, and eat the bread of anxiety. For those beloved of God are given gifts even while they sleep.

Our help is in the name of the eternal God
| who is making the heavens and the earth.

DEAR GOD, thank you for all that is good,
for our creation and our humanity,
for the stewardship you have given us of this planet
    earth,
for the gifts of life and of one another,
for your Love which is unbounded and eternal . . .

O Thou, Most Holy and Beloved,
my Companion, my Unicorn, my Guide upon the Way.

WE repent the wrongs we have done:
our blindness to human need and suffering;
our indifference to injustice and cruelty;
our false judgments, petty thoughts, and contempt;
our waste and pollution of the earth and oceans;
our lack of concern for those who come after us;
our complicity in the making of weapons of mass
    destruction,
and our threatening their use.

Eternal Spirit, living God,
in whom we live and move and have our being,
all that we are, have been, and shall be is known to you,
to the very secrets of our hearts
and all that rises to trouble us.
Living flame, burn into us:
Cleansing wind, blow through us:
Fountain of water, well up within us:
that we may love and praise in deed and in truth.

ETERNAL SPIRIT, flow through our being and open our
    lips
| that our mouths may proclaim your praise.
Let us worship the God of Love:
| Alleluia. Alleluia.

As a deer longs for streams of living water,
so longs my soul for you, O God.
My soul is thirsty for the living God:
when shall I draw near to see your face?
My tears have been my food in the night;
all day long they ask me, Where now is your God?
As I pour out my soul in distress,
I remember how I went to the temple of God,
with shouts and songs of thanksgiving,
a multitude keeping high festival.

Why are you so full of heaviness, my soul,
and why so rebellious within me?
O put your trust in God, patiently wait for the dawn,
and you will then praise your deliverer and your God.

My soul is heavy within me; therefore I remember you
from the land of Jordan and from the hills of Hermon.
Deep calls to deep in the roar of your waterfalls.
All your waves and your torrents have gone over me.

Surely, O God, you will show me mercy in the daytime,
and at night I will sing your praise, O God of my life.
I will say to God, my rock, Why have you forgotten me?
Why must I go like a mourner because the enemy
    oppresses me?
Like a sword piercing my bones, my enemies have
    mocked me,
asking me all day long, Where now is your God?

Why are you so full of heaviness, my soul,
and why so rebellious within me?
O put your trust in God, patiently wait for the dawn,
and you will then praise your deliverer and your God.

O God, take up my cause and strive for me
with a godless people that knows no mercy.
Save me from the grip of cunning and lies,
for you are my God and my strength.
Why have you cast me away from your presence?
Why must I be clothed in rags, humiliated by my
    enemy?
O send out your light and your truth and let them lead
    me,
let them guide me to your holy hill and to your
    dwelling.
Then I shall go to the altar of God, the God of my joy
    and delight,
and to the harp I shall sing your praises, O God my
    God.

Why are you so full of heaviness, my soul,
and why so rebellious within me?
O put your trust in God, patiently wait for the dawn,
and you will then praise your deliverer and your God.

READINGS

*for each day of the month
and for special days
and seasons*

DAY 1. *Poverty:* Miserable are those who crave more and more possessions: they will be crushed by the weight and burden of them. Blessed are those who are ready to do without, to be empty, to be nothing, to be humble and open to receive, knowing their need of God: they have found the secret of living, and are rich indeed.

DAY 2. *Grief:* Miserable are those who wallow in self-pity: they will sink into bitterness and despair. Blessed are those who accept their experience of sorrow: they will grow in courage and compassion.

DAY 3. *Insecurity:* Miserable are those who, in their insecurity, look anxiously for appreciation from others: they claim everything for themselves, and yet possess nothing, wandering unhappily and belonging nowhere. Blessed are those who have accepted their insecurity, and are content to go unrecognised and unrewarded, claiming nothing for themselves: the freedom of the earth is theirs; never exiled, they are everywhere at home.

DAY 4. *Struggle:* Miserable are those who have ceased to care and be disturbed, and are now too much at ease: they will be bored, and will disintegrate into dust. Blessed are those who hunger and thirst and strive for what is just and good: they will be made whole, and will be well content.

DAY 5. *Love:* Miserable are those who show no compassion and are insensitive to the needs of others: they will always complain of being misunderstood and they will never be loved. Blessed are those who accept and forgive those who hurt them: they will find understanding and love.

DAY 6. *Truth:* Miserable are those who live in illusion and fantasy: they will be utterly lost. Blessed are those who are honest with themselves, who are being refined and chastened, and seek to live the truth: they will know themselves and they will know God.

DAY 7. *Peace:* Miserable are those who are at war with themselves, who spread evil and division and hatred, seeking to dominate others: they breed their own downfall and they never know trust and friendship. Blessed are those who create reconciliation and goodwill wherever they go, returning good for evil: they are indeed the friends of God.

DAY 8. *Life:* Miserable are those whose lives are shallow and full of fear, who cannot respond in truth when they are challenged: they will freeze in death. Blessed are those who shed their pettiness, and know the deep things of God and of themselves, and so persevere at whatever the cost – insult, slander, exile, death: they will have life and know it abundantly.

DAY 9. The fruit of the Spirit is love, joy, peace, patience, kindness, goodness, faithfulness, gentleness, self-discipline . . . If we live by the Spirit, let us also walk by the Spirit . . . and bear one another's burdens, and so fulfil the law of Christ.

DAY 10. Love your enemies. Do good to those who hate you. Bless those who curse you. Pray for those who abuse you. Do good and lend, expecting nothing in return. For God is kind to the ungrateful and the selfish. Be merciful as your Father is merciful. Judge not and you will not be judged. Condemn not and you will not be condemned. Forgive and you will be forgiven. Give, and it will be given to you. For the measure you give will be the measure you receive.

DAY 11. Do not ask anxiously, What are we to eat? What are we to drink? What shall we wear? The whole heathen world runs after such things. Set your heart and mind on God's Commonwealth first, and all the rest will come to you as well. So do not be anxious about tomorrow. Today has enough problems of its own; tomorrow can look after itself.

DAY 12. There is no fear in love, but perfect love casts out fear. For fear has to do with punishment, and those who are afraid are not perfected in love. We love because God first loved us. If anyone says, I love God, and hates a brother or sister, that person is a liar; for those who do not love their brothers and sisters whom they have seen cannot love God whom they have not seen.

DAY 13. My food is to do the will of the One who sent me, and to accomplish God's work . . . I have food to eat of which you do not know.

DAY 14. It is the God who said, Let light shine out of darkness, who has shone in our hearts to give the light of the knowledge of the glory of God in the face of Jesus Christ. But we have this treasure in earthen vessels, to show that the transcendent power belongs to God and not to us. We are afflicted in every way, but not crushed; perplexed, but not driven to despair; persecuted, but not forsaken; struck down, but not destroyed; always carrying in the body the death of Jesus, so that the life of Jesus may also be manifested in our bodies.

DAY 15. Living God, you are in the midst of us, and we are called by your holy name; leave us not, O God of Love.

DAY 16. According to the riches of God's glory, may we be strengthened with might through the Holy Spirit in our inner being, and may Christ dwell in our hearts through faith, that, being rooted and grounded in love, we may have power to comprehend, with all the saints, what is the breadth and length and height and depth and to know the love of God which surpasses knowledge, that we may be filled with all the fulness of God.

DAY 17. Those who drink the water that I shall give them shall never thirst: it will become in them a bubbling spring, welling up to eternal life.

DAY 18. God has not given us a spirit of fear, but of power and of love and of a sound mind.

DAY 19. Abide in me and I in you: as the branch cannot bear fruit of itself, unless it abides in the vine, neither can you unless you abide in me . . . Peace I leave with you, my peace I give to you. Let not your hearts be troubled, neither let them be afraid.

DAY 20. All you who are led by the Spirit of God are children of God. For you did not receive the spirit of fear, but you have received the spirit of adoption. When we cry, Abba, Father, it is the Spirit bearing witness with our spirit that we are children of God, and if children, then heirs, heirs of God and fellow heirs with Christ, provided we suffer with Christ that we may also be glorified with him.

DAY 21. This is my commandment, that you love one another, even as I have loved you. Greater love has no one than this, than to lay down one's life for one's friends.

DAY 22. We know that the whole creation itself will be set free from its bondage to decay, having been groaning in travail together until now: and not only the creation, but we ourselves, who have the first fruits of the Spirit, groan inwardly as we wait for our adoption as sons and daughters, the redemption of our bodies, and obtain the glorious liberty of the children of God.

DAY 23. I am sure that neither death nor life, nor angels, nor principalities nor powers, nor things present nor things to come, nor height nor depth, nor anything else in all creation will be able to separate us from the love of God in Christ Jesus.

DAY 24. The God who calls you is faithful. The same God will enable you, fulfilling the promise of old.

DAY 25. Though our outer nature is wasting away, our inner nature is being renewed every day. For this slight momentary affliction is preparing for us an eternal weight of glory beyond comparison, because we look not to the things that are seen, but to the things that are unseen; for the things that are seen are transient, but the things that are unseen are eternal.

DAY 26. Open your mouth for the dumb, for the rights of those who are left desolate. Open your mouth, judge righteously, maintain the rights of the poor and needy.

DAY 27. The Spirit of God is upon me, anointing me to preach good news to the poor, sending me to proclaim release to the captives and recovering of sight to the blind, to set at liberty those who are oppressed, to proclaim the time of God's grace and favour.

DAY 28. There is great gain in godliness with contentment. For we brought nothing into this world and we cannot take anything out of it. But if we have food and clothing, with these we shall be content . . . For the love of money is the root of all evils . . . So shun all this: aim at justice, Christlikeness, fidelity, steadfastness, gentleness.

DAY 29. Let not the foreigner who has joined himself to Yahweh say, You will surely separate me from your people. And let not the eunuch say, Behold, I am a dry tree. For thus says Yahweh, To the eunuchs who keep my sabbaths, who choose the things that please me and hold fast to my covenant, I will give in my house and within my walls a monument and a name better than sons and daughters: I will give them an everlasting name which shall not be cut off. And to the foreigners also who join themselves to me, to minister to me, to love my name, and to be my servants . . . I will make them joyful in my house of prayer, and their sacrifices will be accepted on my altar, for my house shall be called a house of prayer for all peoples. For thus says Yahweh, who gathers the outcasts of Israel, I will gather others to me besides those already gathered.

DAY 30. I may have the gift of many languages and of great eloquence, but if I have no love in my heart, I am but a hollow gong or a clashing cymbal. I may be a man of God, and understand and explain every hidden truth, but if I have no love, I am nothing. I may have faith strong enough to move mountains, I may give away all that I have to feed the hungry, I may even seek the glory of a martyr, but if I have no love, I achieve precisely nothing.

Love is patient and kind and knows no envy. Love never clings, is never boastful, conceited, or rude. Love is never selfish, never insists on its own way. Love is not quick to take offence. Love keeps no score of wrongs, nor gloats over the sins of others. Love rejoices in the truth. Love is tough: there

is nothing it cannot face. Love never loses trust in human
beings or in God. Love never loses hope, never loses heart.
Love still stands when all else has fallen. For everything else
will vanish, prophecy, knowledge, ecstasy. For these are all
partial, and will cease when fulfilment comes. When I grew
to be a man, I put away childish things: so now we see only
puzzling reflections in a mirror, but then we shall see face to
face. Now I know but little of the truth. Then my knowledge
will be whole, like God's knowledge of me. In a word, but
three things last for ever: faith, hope, and love. And it is love
that crowns them all.

DAY 31. You are no longer strangers and sojourners, but
fellow citizens with the saints, and members of the household
of God, built upon the foundation of the apostles and pro-
phets: Jesus Christ is the cornerstone, in whom the whole
structure is joined together and grows into a holy temple of
God: in whom also we are built into it for a dwelling place of
God in the Spirit.

Advent   A voice cries, In the wilderness prepare the
                way of Yahweh: make straight in the desert a
                highway for our God. Every valley shall be
                lifted up, and every mountain and hill made
                low: the uneven ground shall become level,
                and the rough places a plain. And the glory of
                Yahweh shall be revealed, and all flesh shall
                see it together.

Christmas   The Word became flesh and dwelt among us,
                full of grace and truth. We beheld the glory of
                God shining through a human face – as a
                mother's eyes live through her daughter's and
                as a son reflects his father's image – the glory
                of God in a human being fully alive.

Epiphany   Our eyes have seen your salvation, which you have prepared for all peoples, a light to enlighten the nations, and give glory to your people Israel.

Lent   Is not this the fast that I choose: to loose the bonds of wickedness, to undo the thong of the yoke, to let the oppressed go free, and to break every prison bar? Is it not to share your bread with the hungry, and to bring the homeless poor into your house: when you see the naked, to cover him, and not to hide yourself from your own flesh? Then shall your light break forth as the dawn, and your healing shall spring up speedily.

Passiontide   He was scourged for our faults, he was bruised for our sins. On him lies the chastisement that makes us whole, and with his wounds we are healed.

Easter   Christ is risen from the dead, and become the first fruits of those who slept. As death came into the world by a human being, so also has come the resurrection of the dead. For as in Adam all die, even so in Christ shall all be made alive.

Ascension   Christ reigns! He disarmed the principalities and powers, he triumphed over evil and pain and death. He is with us always, to the end of time.

Pentecost   The love of God has been shed abroad in our
                hearts through the Holy Spirit who has been
                given to us . . . For God has not given us a
                spirit of fear, but of power and of love and of a
                sound mind.

Trinity   Voices of countless angels praise you, myriads
                upon myriads, thousands upon thousands,
                sing to you with ceaseless praise: Holy, holy,
                holy is God the sovereign ruler of all, who was
                and who is and who is to come, Amen.
                Blessing and glory and wisdom and thanks-
                giving and power and love to be our God for
                ever and ever.

Saints' Days These are the words of the First and the Last,
                who was dead and came to life again: To
                those who are victorious I will give the right
                to eat from the tree of life that stands in the
                Garden of God, alleluia. Be faithful to death,
                and I will give you the crown of life, alleluia.
                To those who are victorious I will give some
                of the hidden manna, I will give them also a
                white stone, alleluia. And on the stone will be
                written a new name, known only to the one
                who receives it, alleluia.

The Departed Thanks be to God, because in Christ's victory
                over the grave a new age has dawned, the
                long reign of sin is over, a broken world is
                being renewed, and we are once again made
                whole. As we believe that Jesus died and rose
                again, so we believe it will be for those who
                have died: God will bring them to life with
                Christ Jesus.

HYMNS

SUNDAY

HAIL, gladdening Light, of God's pure glory poured,
Who is the great Creator, heavenly, blest,
Holiest of holies, Jesus Christ who reigns.

Now we are come to the sun's hour of rest,
The lights of evening round us shine,
We hymn the God of Love, Eternal Spirit divine.

You are worthy, O God, at all times to be sung
With clear and truthful voice,
Light of Light, Giver of life, alone!
Therefore in all the world your glories, Christ, they own.

MONDAY

GLORY to you, my God, this night,
For all the blessings of the light,
To you, from whom all good does come,
Our life, our health, our lasting home.

Teach me to live, that I may dread
The grave as little as my bed,
Teach me to die, that so I may
Rise glorious at the aweful day.

O may I now on you repose,
And may kind sleep my eyelids close,
Sleep that may me more vigorous make
To serve my God when I awake.

If I lie restless on my bed,
Your word of healing peace be said,
If powerful dreams rise in the night,
Transform their darkness into light.

All praise to God, sustaining us,
Redeeming and transfiguring us,
Thanksgiving in eternity,
All praise, beloved Trinity.

TUESDAY

GUIDE me, O thou great Redeemer,
Pilgrim through this barren land,
I am weak, but thou art mighty,
Hold me with thy powerful hand:
    Bread of heaven,
Feed me now and evermore.

Open now the crystal fountain,
Whence the healing stream doth flow;
Let the fiery, cloudy pillar
Lead me all my journey through:
    Strong Deliverer,
Be thou still my strength and shield.

When I tread the verge of Jordan,
Bid my anxious fears subside,
Death of death, and hell's destruction,
Land me safe on Canaan's side:
    Songs and praises
I will ever give to thee.

WEDNESDAY

BEFORE the ending of the day,
Creator of the world we pray,
That you, with love and lasting light,
Would guard us through the hours of night,

From all ill dreams defend our eyes,
From nightly fears and fantasies,
Redeem through us our evil foe,
That we no lasting harm may know.

O Wisest Guide, grant all we ask,
Fulfil in us your holy task,
Surround us with your love and care,
And lead us on, your life to share.

All praise to God, sustaining us,
Redeeming and transfiguring us,
Thanksgiving in eternity,
All praise, beloved Trinity.

THURSDAY

BE thou my vision, O Christ of my heart,
Be all else but naught to me save that thou art,
Be thou my best thought in the day and the night,
Both waking and sleeping, thy presence my light.

Riches I heed not, nor vain empty praise,
Be thou my inheritance now and always,
Be thou and thou only the first in my heart,
O Sovereign of heaven, my treasure thou art.

FRIDAY

O THOU who camest from above,
The fire celestial to impart,
Kindle a flame of sacred love
On the low altar of my heart.

There let it for thy glory burn
With inextinguishable blaze,
And trembling to its source return
In humble prayer and fervent praise.

Jesus confirm my heart's desire
To work and speak and think for thee,
Still let me guard the holy fire,
And still stir up thy gift in me.

Ready for all thy perfect will,
My acts of faith and love repeat,
Till death thine endless mercies seal,
And make the sacrifice complete.

SATURDAY

Be still in God's Presence,
Be still in God's Presence,
Be still in God's Presence,
   And love and be loved.　　*(Repeat)*

Fall deep in the silence,
Fall deep in the silence,
Fall deep in the silence,
   The silence of God.　　*(Repeat)*

PRAYERS

INTO YOUR HANDS

INTO your hands, O God, I commend my spirit,
| for you have redeemed me, O God of truth and love.
Keep me, O God, as the apple of an eye:
| hide me under the shadow of your wings.

ANTIPHONS TO NUNC DIMITTIS

Advent
Come, O God, and visit us in peace; that we may rejoice in your presence with a perfect heart.

Christmas
Alleluia. The Word was made flesh, alleluia, and dwelt among us, alleluia, alleluia.

Epiphany
Alleluia, All nations shall come before God, alleluia. And they will glorify God's holy name, alleluia, alleluia.

Lent
For their sake I consecrate myself, that they also may be consecrated in truth.

Passiontide
Christ became obedient to death, even death on a cross.

Easter
Alleluia. Christ is risen, alleluia. He is risen indeed, alleluia, alleluia.

Ascension
Alleluia. The pioneer of our salvation has triumphed through suffering and death, alleluia. The firstborn among many sisters and brothers has led the way into the presence of God, alleluia, alleluia.

Pentecost
Alleluia. The Holy Spirit will teach you all things, alleluia. And will guide you into all truth, alleluia, alleluia.

Trinity   Alleluia. Great praise and everlasting glory be to God, Sustainer, Redeemer, Sanctifier, alleluia. Alpha and Omega, the beginning and the end, alleluia, alleluia.

Saints' Days   Alleluia. The Lamb who was slain has conquered, alleluia. All who follow the Way will share in the victory, alleluia, alleluia.

Ordinary Days Preserve us, O God, while waking, and guard us while sleeping, that awake we may watch with Christ, and asleep may rest in your peace.

NUNC DIMITTIS

PRAISE be to God, I have lived to see this day.
God's promise is fulfilled, and my duty done.

At last you have given me peace,
for I have seen with my own eyes
the salvation you have prepared for all nations –
a light to the world in its darkness,
and the glory of your people Israel.

Glory be to God, sustaining, redeeming, sanctifying,
as in the beginning, so now, and for ever. Amen.

KYRIES

KYRIE eleison
| Christe eleison
Kyrie eleison

LORD'S PRAYER

ETERNAL Spirit,
Life-Giver, Pain-Bearer, Love-Maker,
Source of all that is and that shall be,
Father and Mother of us all,
Loving God, in whom is heaven:

The Hallowing of your Name
  echo through the universe!
The Way of your Justice
  be followed by the peoples of the world!
Your Heavenly Will
  be done by all created beings!
Your Commonwealth of Peace and Freedom
  sustain our hope and come on earth!

With the bread we need for today,
  feed us.
In the hurts we absorb from one another,
  forgive us.
In times of temptation and test,
  strengthen us.
From trials too great to endure,
  spare us.
From the grip of all that is evil,
  free us.

For you reign in the glory
of the power that is love,
now and for ever. Amen.

I WILL LIE DOWN IN PEACE

I will lie down in peace and take my rest,
| for it is in God alone that I dwell unafraid.
Let us bless the Life-Giver, the Pain-Bearer, the Love-
Maker,
| let us praise and exalt God above all for ever.
May God's name be praised beyond the furthest star,
| glorified and exalted above all for ever.

O LIVING GOD

O living God, in Jesus Christ you were laid in the tomb at
this evening hour, and so sanctified the grave to be a bed of
hope to your people. Give us courage and faith to die daily
to our sin and pride, that even as this flesh and blood decays,
our lives still may grow in you, that at our last day our dying
may be done so well that we live in you for ever.

ADDITIONAL PRAYERS
FOR EACH DAY OF THE MONTH

[1] For all that has been, thanks. To all that shall be, yes. At
all times and in all places.

[2] Loving God, bless us and those you have entrusted to
us . . . Fill us with the Spirit of the Beatitudes. keep us
simple, joyful, and full of mercy.

[3] Rejoice, Mary, you are full of God's grace, the Lord is
with you. You are blessed among women, and Jesus your
child is blessed: and in him are blessed . . . Holy Mary,
Mother of God, pray for us sinners, now and at the hour of
our death.

[4] Watch between us, dear God, when we are absent from
one another.

[5] Eternal God, Giver of all good gifts, we your friends and servants now give you humble and hearty thanks for all your goodness and loving kindness to us and to all folk. We bless you for our creation, preservation, and all the blessings of this life . . . but above all for your inestimable love in the redemption of the world by our Saviour Jesus Christ, for the means of grace and for the hope of glory . . . And we ask of you, give us that due sense of all your mercies, that our hearts may be unreservedly thankful, and that we show forth your praise, not only with our lips but in our lives, by giving up ourselves to your service, and by walking before you in holiness and righteousness all our days; through Jesus Christ our Redeemer, to whom with you and the Holy Spirit, be all honour and glory, world without end.

[6] We adore thee, who art One and who art Love; and it is in unity and love that we would live together, doing thy will.

[7] Kristos, Kristopheros, friend and brother, give mercy, healing, peace.
  [Kristos, Wise Guardian, ancient and young, the Other Within, yet needing me to bear my crucial part, Kristopheros]

[8] In this life and beyond, with our ancestors of the flesh, in company with the saints, in love for those we have known, all glory and praise to God.

[9] Old and young, women and men, black and white, your people, God, one Church. Rich and poor, oppressed and free, disobedient and faithful, your people, God, one World.

[10] O God of many names, Lover of all peoples, we pray for peace, in our hearts, in our homes, in our nations, in our world, the peace of your will, the peace of our need.

[11] Divine Lover,
   so fill me with yourself that I may be all love.
Transform my self-centredness
in your penetrating love and compassion.

In the power of your love dwelling in me,
may I now radiate
   Love . . .
   Compassion . . .
   Joy . . .
   Peace . . .

Within this radiation of love I place
   my family . . .
   my friends . . .
   my colleagues . . .
   those who have trusted me with their secrets . . .
   those whom I love and like . . .
   those whom I cannot yet like . . .
   those who are my enemies . . .
   those to whom are entrusted power, influence,
      decision . . .
   those in trouble . . . sorrow . . . anxiety . . . illness . . .
   those who are jubilant . . .
   those who are quietly contented . . .
   those who are dying . . .
   those who have died . . .
   all humankind . . .
   all creation . . .

Divine Lover,
whom the heavens adore,
may the whole earth worship you,
all tongues confess you,
all peoples obey you,
and all your friends love and serve you
in unity, trust, and peace.

[12] "He fed them according to the integrity of his heart, and guided them by the skilfulness of his hands." May we so counsel one another.

[13] *Refrain:* O God, save your people.
From the Spirit of Force . . .
From Greed for Gain . . .
From the Risk of War . . .
From Weapons of Slaughter . . .
From the Military Mind . . .
From the Destroyers . . .
From our own Indifference . . .
From Bitter Hatred . . .
From Ruthless and Dangerous Men . . .
From Blind Obedience to Authority . . .
From Unwillingness to See or Think or Discern . . .

[14] O God, the Source of the whole world's gladness and the bearer of its pain, may your unconquerable joy rest at the heart of all our trouble and distress.

[15] O God, you have prepared for those who love you such good things as pass our understanding; pour into our hearts such love towards you, that loving you both in all things and above all things, we may inherit your promises, which exceed all that we can desire, in Jesus Christ, ever-loving and ever-beloved.

[16] Holy Spirit, Counsellor and Strengthener of all who put their trust in you, grant that we may both perceive and know the things we ought to do, and also have grace and power faithfully to fulfil the same.

[17] Most merciful Redeemer, Friend and Brother, may we know you more clearly, love you more dearly, and follow your more nearly, day by day.

[18] O God, you have taught us that all that we do is worth nothing without your self-giving love; send your Holy Spirit and pour into our hearts that most excellent gift of love, the very bond of peace and of all virtues, without which all who live are counted as dead before you. We pray this in and through the One who showed us Love, Jesus Christ our Saviour.

[19] God of all power and might, author and giver of all good things, graft in our hearts the love of your name, increase in us true religion, nourish us with all goodness, and of your great mercy keep us in the same.

[20] O God, strengthen your servants with your heavenly grace, that we may continue yours for ever, and daily increase in your Holy Spirit more and more, until we come to your everlasting Kingdom.

[21] Almighty God, who alone can order the unruly wills and affections of sinful folk, grant to your people, that they may love the things which you command and desire that which you promise, that so, among the many and varied changes of the world, our hearts may surely there be fixed, where true joys are to be found.

[22] May fruitless strife and ruinous wars pass away and may the Great Peace come. Let us not glory in this, that we love our country, let us rather glory in this, that we love our human kind.

[23] Eternal God, in whose perfect realm no sword is drawn but the sword of justice, and no strength known but the strength of love, so guide and inspire the work of all who seek your commonwealth, that all peoples may seek and find their security, not in force of arms but in the perfect love that casts our fear and in the fellowship revealed to us in Jesus Christ.

[24] Give me, O God, ears to hear that the flute of the universe is played without ceasing, and that its sound is love.

[25] God bless [Africa]: guard her children, guide her rulers, and give her peace.

[26] Loving God, in Jesus Christ you yearn to bring the whole world to the glorious liberty of the children of God. Open the eyes of the oppressor and torturer to the blindness of their injustice. Open the way of freedom for those in prison for what they believe. Anoint us with the Spirit of Christ to make us servants of the oppressed and instruments of your power, so that justice and peace may embrace and your love rule in the hearts of all folk.

[27] O just and holy God, you have brought us peace by making the many peoples into one people, Jew and Gentile, slave and free, male and female, black and white. We pray for those places where peoples are kept apart because of the colour of their skin. Help us to root out discrimination in our hearts so that we may welcome every stranger in our midst as a fellow citizen, a neighbour, and a friend of God.

[28] O God, give us courage to stand up and be counted, to stand up for those who cannot do so for themselves, and to stand up for ourselves when it is needful for us to do so. Let us fear nothing more than we fear you, and let us love nothing more than we love you – for thus we shall fear nothing also. Let us have no other God before you, whether nation or party or state or church. Let us seek no other peace but your peace, and make us its instruments, opening our eyes and ears and hearts, so that we should always know what work of peace we may do for you.

[29] O God, from whom all holy desires, all good counsels, and all just works do proceed, give unto thy servants that peace which the world cannot give, that our hearts may be set to obey thy commandments, and also that by thee, we, being defended from the fear of our enemies, may pass our time in rest and quietness; through the merits of Jesus Christ our Saviour.

[30] Lighten our darkness, we ask of you, dear God, and in your great mercy strengthen us to face all perils and dangers of the night; for the love of your only Son our Saviour Jesus Christ.

[31] O God, open my eyes that I may see the needs of others, open my ears that I may hear their cries, open my heart so that they need not be without compassion. Let me not be afraid to defend the weak because of the anger of the strong, nor afraid to defend the poor because of the anger of the rich. Show me where love and hope and faith are needed, and use me to bring them to these places. Open my eyes and ears that I may, this coming day, do some work of peace for you.

FINAL PRAYER

BE present, Living Christ, within us,
your dwelling place and home,
that this house may be one where
all darkness is penetrated by your light,
all troubles calmed by your peace,
all evil redeemed by your love,
all pain transformed in your suffering.
and all dying glorified in your risen life.

OR

Be present, Spirit of God,
and renew us through the silent hours of this night,
so that we who are wearied by the changes and chances
    of this fleeting world,
may rest upon your eternal changelessness;
in the Spirit of Jesus Christ,
our Guardian and our Guide.

BLESSING

Sunday O God of love and mercy, grant us, with all your people, rest and peace.

Monday God bless us and keep us, God's face shine on us and be gracious to us, and give us light and peace.

Tuesday To God the Creator who loved us first and gave this world to be our home, to God the Redeemer who loves us and by dying and rising pioneered the way of freedom, to God the Sanctifier who spreads the divine love in our hearts, be praise and glory for time and for eternity.

Wednesday The grace of Jesus Christ, the love of God, and communion in the Holy Spirit, be with us now and always.

Thursday The blessing of God, Life-Giver, Pain-Bearer, Love-Maker, be with us now and always.

Friday The blessing of God, the eternal goodwill of God, the shalom of God, the wildness and the warmth of God, be among us and between us, now and always.

Saturday Blessing, light, and glory surround us and scatter the darkness of the long and lonely night.

The divine Spirit dwells in us:
| Thanks be to God.

That Night and Day
shall be a single whole

Cairns for a journey

BE open to the night . . .

Pray with open hand, not with clenched fist . . .

Shapes loom out of the darkness, uncertain and unclear: but the hooded stranger on horseback emerging from the mist need not be assumed to be the bearer of ill . . .

The night is large and full of wonders . . .   [1]

✢

DIG deep through unrelenting earth . . .
Trudge through cloying mud . . .

There is gold to be mined . . .
There are diamonds to be distilled . . .

In the hardest rock of fate there is a thin vein of mercy . . .
In the grinding small of pebbles there is a sparse hope . . . [2]

PEOPLE like you must *look* at everything and *think* about it and communicate with the heaven that dwells deep within them and listen inwardly for a word to come.   [3]

✢

To embark on an adventure is to be up against it – 'advenio': to come against. The way cannot be seen clearly . . .

It is an ancient unknown, silent and dark . . .   [4]

But to enter the darkness in trust is to emerge more whole . . .

To go further into the inner caverns of badness and self-hatred, with steadiness and courage, is to emerge into a broad place . . .

a place of greater honesty and clarity in encounters with others . . .

a place of greater willingness to meet others who are very different . . .

a place of greater ability and enjoyment in loving and being loved by friends . . .

a place of greater strength and compassion . . .

❖

GIVE me a candle of the Spirit, O God, as I go down into the deeps of my being. Show me the hidden things, the creatures of my dreams, the storehouse of forgotten memories and hurts. Take me down to the spring of my life, and tell me my nature and my name. Give me freedom to grow, so that I may become that self, the seed of which you planted in me at my making. Out of the deeps I cry to you, O God. [5]

❖

THE frontiers of the familiar are closed to you: you have no resting place there . . . [6]

You *have* to be a pioneer, journeying to places which the rest of the world ignores, humbly and courageously opening yourself to what others do not wish to see, both good and evil . . .

It *is* a wilderness: but take it to your heart and bless it . . . [7]

It *is* a narrow way: but do not complain – the Way chose you, and you must be thankful . . . [8]

It *is* a difficult choice, but to choose what is difficult as if it were easy, *that* is faith . . . [9]

Do not retreat from the unfamiliar, nor condemn it. When a civilisation turns, God may not be found at the old landmarks . . . [10]

❖

LISTEN . . .

to the fragile feelings, not to the clashing fury . . .

to the quiet sounds, not to the loud clamour . . .

to the steady heartbeat, not to the noisy confusion . . .

to the hidden voices, not to the obvious chatter . . .

to the deep harmonies, not to the surface discord . . .

❖

LISTEN . . .

to the outcast within you . . .

the only one whence healing and reconciliation come . . .

the only one who can bring salvation to the part of you that speaks loudest and thinks itself strongest . . .

In your inscape, as well as in the landscape of the wider world, the voice of the poor and the oppressed has priority over the voice of the dominant . . .   [11]

We must not refuse to become aware of all that we find distressing or painful or fearful within: if we do, we shall merely project onto others our own inner darkness . . .

Are you white and afraid of your blackness? . . .

Are you male and afraid of the feminine within? . . .

Are you heterosexual and afraid of your homosexual feelings? . . .

Are you rich and afraid of your poverty? . . .

Are you young and afraid of being old? . . .

Are you healthy and afraid of your mortality? . . .

Are you able and afraid of disability? . . .

Are you busily involved and afraid of being useless? . . .

Nothing is to be expelled as foreign . . .

All is to be befriended and transformed . . .

❖

Be patient toward all that is unsolved in your heart . . .

Try to love the questions themselves . . .

Do not now seek the answers, which cannot be given because you would not be able to live them . . .

Live the questions now. Perhaps you will then gradually, without noticing it, live along some distant day into the answers . . .   [12]

❖

To assuage the hunger pains that arise in our loneliness we grab, *reacting* immediately . . .

Rather pause . . . become still . . . be patient . . . love yourself . . . lay on one side all self-hatred . . .

Only in this way do we begin to *respond* from a place of inner truth . . .

asking, not grabbing, no longer crushed by a *refusal* . . . [13]

Taste – pause – and only then spit or swallow . . .

❖

ILL at ease, discontented, restless – we name the feeling
'loneliness' and seek to escape from it into comfort or
excitement . . .

Stop . . . acknowledge the true name of the feeling as a thirst
and desire for God . . .

Stay with the painfully awakened desire for the Mysterious
Companion, the Other Within . . .

Only God can lift us out of our enslavement, our estrange-
ment, our displacedness . . .

No human being, just as lonely as we are, can do this for
us . . .

Only in knowing our worth, our specialness, our significance
in God is the resource for genuinely moving outwards towards
others . . .

You cannot *make* yourself special: you just *are* special . . .

Out of openness to the Other Within flows a universal
loving, a loving which does not see a stranger as a threat, nor
demands everything of intimacy, so turning delight into a
burden . . .   [14]

❖

IN solitude *love* is known . . .

Do not be afraid of being or living alone . . .

There is a hermit in each of us: perhaps there is room in this
world only for hermits – or at most hermits in pairs . . . [15]

It is a deep love, that of two solitudes who protect and greet
and touch each other . . .   [16]

❖

LISTEN to the language of your wounds . . .

Do not pine away in the pain of your wounds, but live from the depth of them, making the extent of your desolation the extent of your realm . . .   [17]

We cannot avoid suffering, but we can grow through suffering in a way that we can't with success . . .

The fruits of striving with difficulty and failure last longer than those that come with ease . . .

To have suffered – this can never be taken away, whether it leads to bitterness or to compassion . . .

So does the wounded oyster transform grit to pearl . . . [18]

There is something in us which does not yet exist, and our hearts are wounded, even broken, in order that it may have existence . . .   [19]

The tensions remain, but these may be used to play tunes that otherwise nobody could have heard. Would we deny ourselves that high calling for the sake of ease – or even of happiness? . . .   [20]

The wounded frightened child within you needs your adult caring strength, so that the gift he/she is protecting may be yours . . .

We sometimes fear to draw close to another because our early intrinsic tenderness has been violated . . .

Seek your hurt child in unending wastes, where he/she waits to speak to you of Long Ago in the language of wounds . . .
                                                      [21]

❖

IF you take away my pain, you take away my passion . . .

By all means share my pain – and share yours with me, but do not lie and pretend you can make it disappear . . .

For the pain is *mine*, and I want to mould it, to shape it, to use this very raw material to create – 'glory'. There are no words for it, for it has not yet been born . . .

And it is part of *our* pain – and glory – part of the world's pain which has not yet been transformed, and which we can but shuffle round a little . . .

The more I can bear my own, go with its grain, the more I can share yours, as you lead me into your dark cave . . .

The pain of the world will not cease until its dark places have been penetrated with light, the light of understanding that uses the power of the dark to *create* . . .

And that will not happen until we all come together to acknowledge the pain, to understand, to create . . .

Until then, each glimpse I have of joy and healing throws into sharp relief the pain of others, bearable to them only if the scars can still be seen, their ache still there in a rich compassion.

> Drink deep of the chalice of grief and sorrow,
> held out to you by your dark angel of Gethsemane:
> the angel is not your enemy,
> the drink, though sharp, is nourishing,
> by which you may come to a deeper peace
> than if you pass it by,
> a 'health of opened heart' . . .   [22]

❖

FROM a slow accepting of our wounds, life within us begins to move outward, bitterness waning, compassion growing . . .

True prayer is the source, the prayer that comes not from the mouth, but as from the lips of wounds . . .   [23]

Hidden in that prayer is both the crucified Christ and our
fellow sufferers, those whom, in intercession and compassion,
we need in order to be ourselves.

There is no higher aim
　　than to reclaim
another, blinded by life's pain,
　　to help him live and see again.　　　　[24]

Seek love in the pity of another's woe,
In the gentle relief of another's care,
In the darkness of night and the winter's snow,
In the naked and outcast – seek love there.　　　[25]

❖

MAY our only wounds be these:
　　the wound that we cannot avoid
　　because we belong to one another,
　　and feel and hear the murmur of the world's pain;
　　the wound of a sense of compassion for others;
　　the wound of a sense of longing for God,
　　the Source of Life and Love
　　deep within us and far beyond us.　　　[26]

❖

LOVE your body . . .

You are a body:
not a no-body,
nor just any-body,
but some-body . . .

And we are a Body,
and we are the Body of Christ . . .

The Body is the dwelling-place
of the whole-making Spirit . . .

You are a body in the milieu of Spirit . . .

GOD accepts you as you are . . .

God has created you a sexual being . . .

God is at the heart of your striving,
still creating you,
now as lover in the image of Divine Love . . .

always pursuing, luring, drawing,
never letting go . . .

Whatever your unique mix and measure of sexuality, be very glad: to be a human sexual is fundamental and ordinary and exceptional . . .

And because we are loved unconditionally,
we don't have to take ourselves too seriously . . .

If I were the finger of God,
and all the world were ticklish . . .

❖

GOD be in my head and in my understanding
God be in my eyes and in my looking
God be in my mouth and in my speaking
God be in my tongue and in my tasting
God be in my lips and in my greeting

God be in my nose and in my smelling/inhaling
God be in my ears and in my hearing
God be in my neck and in my humbling
God be in my shoulders and in my bearing
God be in my back and in my standing

God be in my arms and in my reaching/receiving
God be in my hands and in my working
God be in my legs and in my walking
God be in my feet and in my grounding
God be in my joints and in my relating

God be in my guts and in my feeling
God be in my bowels and in my forgiving
God be in my loins and in my swiving
God be in my lungs and in my breathing
God be in my heart and in my loving

God be in my skin and in my touching
God be in my flesh and in my paining/pining
God be in my blood and in my living
God be in my bones and in my dying
God be at my end and at my reviving

❖

WHEN we come to the place of our *wounded* sexuality, healing cannot start from the place of passion . . .

The temptation is to cut off from the ache of the wound and search desperately for sensation . . .

Rather must the search be for other moments of bodily loving and touch, assured of another's steady love . . .

> . . . small healing sacraments of touch,
> where loneliness is relieved,
> where delight is shared,
> where flesh is comforted,
> where sleep may come in another's arms . . .

Only then, bodies deeply affirmed as good, can mightier moments of passion be contained . . .

Without the ground bass of the quieter moments, the louder ones, like exploding shells, destroy or freeze, body-blows that shock . . .

In the place of our wounding 'in the groin',
by rejection of our sexuality,
by rejection of our bodily self,
by a physical wound to the flesh,
healing cannot come by way of a passionate falling-in-
    loveness,
however much its siren strains try to convince us . . .

Only deep love and gentle touch and steady goodwill can
heal . . .

If the wounding is so deep that we can never reach the point
where passion can be contained, we have to be loyal to these
other ways of healing, and when we are, *just as much love is
made* . . .

There are dark times when this is not believable, when even
the sustaining love of others cannot be received, however
much it is offered and yearned for . . .

. . . The *experience* of love is then far distant, and the
temptation is to despair . . .

. . . All that can be done is to cleave to hope, loyally bearing
the wounds, gently probing them, living and delving the
space between ourselves and others . . .

. . . Then, at unlooked-for moments of meeting, the touch of
a finger is enough to create a universe . . .   [27]

For there *is* the dearest freshness deep down things . . . [28]

❖

WE are destined to be makers of love,
passionately or tenderly,
focused genitally or more diffused . . .

The most loving sexual act of all is gently to reach for
another and through touch make that person feel whole . . .

                                              [29]

After the making of love you feel that you have had a bath, not that you need one . . .

Our regrets should be about those we haven't touched, those we have neglected to say and show that we loved them. The commandment is this: Go forth and touch . . . Thou shalt not commit unloving . . .   [30]

So the creative Spirit is released in us, whatever shape that Spirit may take on emerging . . .

So we live the life of God, the God who is an intimacy in our flesh which otherwise is death . . .   [31]

✤

O GOD,
Giver of life,
Bearer of pain,
Maker of love,
affirming in your incarnation the goodness of the flesh,
may the yearnings of our bodies
be fulfilled in sacraments of love,
and our earthly embracings
a foretaste of the glory that shall be,
in the light of Resurrection of Jesus Christ . . .

✤

WHEN fear comes, pause . . .
Say what you are afraid of . . .
Feel the fear . . .
Take time . . .
Then the barrier to trust will be lower,
the jump to be taken no longer paralysing,
Have courage . . .
The Presence is very close and very loving . . .

✤

WE constantly exhort one another to be good,
and just as constantly we fail . . .
Realise this and give it up . . .
Guilt and fear drive out the love we seek,
allies of a cold moralism, rigid and solemn . . .

Accept the truth that you fail . . .
Admit the shams and pretence and lying and pride . . .
Accept that much failure comes from love not knowing
   how to love well . . .
Relax . . .
Let laughter well up from the depths of your being . . .
Let tears well up too . . .
Shake away the fear and become warm and flowing . . .

❖

'WORDS of God'? Forgive me for having created a world in
which so much pain has to be allowed to happen if I am
truly to be a God of Love and enable you to love with a love
that is worthy of the name . . .   [32]

❖

WHEN we receive the forgiveness of another,
the depths of our personalities are disturbed.
For it means that the worst in us has been accepted –
and that means a kind of death.
We have no need to fight our own worst selves any
   more.
And it is hard to receive this truth.
We turn against our forgiver in self-justification.
How dare you accept me as I am and not condemn me?
So folk turned against Christ for so accepting them.
But God's forgiveness is without condition.
It sweeps us off our feet.
We want to make conditions,
so that there can be a core still under our control.

To let go completely –
this is death –
but it is necessary if we are to find life.
To let go into God –
this is death.
So receiving forgiveness is to prepare ourselves for the
    final letting go,
for the decisive moment of truth,
by a little dying,
a little letting go.

❖

To be saved is to be so enlarged as to have space and
spaciousness to fight lovingly with our enemies, that they
may be embraced in friendship . . .

Love your enemies:
do not condemn, do not destroy . . .

Keep in contact,
even if you cannot keep 'in touch' . . .

Strive powerfully with your enemies,
struggle shoulder to shoulder,
and then see each other face to face . . .

Do not yield to bitterness, nor to despair,
nor to the violence that does nothing but destroy . . .

Do not dismiss even your worst enemy as inhuman . . .

Beloved enemy . . .

Be generously angry,
and let your compassion be felt behind your anger, not
    your hatred . . .

[Dissolve the hatred by believing deep
in your own heart that *you are indeed loved* . . .]

Love with an expanding heart . . .

Do not meet oppression with force,
for we have all been too much hurt . . .

Be powerfully and persuasively gentle –
with others and with yourself . . .

And keep a sense of proportion,
and a sense of humour . . .

❖

THE fauna of the night,
hidden in the grass of your neglect . . .

encounter them . . .
contemplate them . . .
dare to look steadily at them . . .
wrestle with them . . .
expect to be wounded in the struggle with them . . .
name them . . .
recognise them . . .
and be blessed by them . . .

At the breaking of dawn
they will be know as delectable creatures,
no longer exiled,   [33]
but returned to you,
made precious again,
moving with you into the future,
robed as destinies . . .   [34]

Within us and among us and through the world
there are many powers of dis-ease which entangle us . . .

They grip us, trouble us, distract us, wound us . . .

They go by many names:
greed, pride, malice, envy, evil,
grief, rage, fear, pain, death . . .

some known in the secret places of our hearts . . .
some as yet unknown to us . . .
some greater in strength than any one of us can bear
    alone . . .

✛

"In the name of God,
in the name of Jesus Christ,
come out of darkness into light,
that we may understand and withstand you,
that we may know your name and nature,
that you may cease your hold on us
and wound us no more,
and be transformed by the power of that Love
that is deeper than the deepest pain,
yielding your energy in the service of God . . ."

So may we be freed to be the friends of God,
and live to reflect God's glory . . .

✛

You are troubled by your dark angels . . .
You seek to tame their wildness . . .
But they are the potential source of creativity within
    you . . .
If you deny them, banish them, seek to destroy them,
they will drain you of passion as they retreat,
and you will become pale and lifeless . . .
And if they should return and storm your gates,
you would then be destroyed . . .
However dark, they are still angels,
guardians and protectors too . . .   [35]

BE in love with life,
wrestle with the chaos and the pain,
with your self and with others,
spirit echoing Spirit,
trusting in the victory of the vulnerable,
glimpsing the peace,
the wholeness,
the spaciousness,
the justice,
and the joy
that comes from following the Pioneer
made perfect in suffering,
striving and yearning and crying out
from the very depths and heights
of the world's anguish and the world's bliss,
and so becoming friends and partners of God
in the divine creating . . .

❖

BE not stiff-necked but yield yourself . . .
Let God direct your bodily being . . .
Let the Spirit flow through you . . .

You will then be relaxed,
and the government will be upon God's shoulders . . .

Those who hold on to their life will lose it . . .
Those who let go of their life will find it . . .

Let go . . .
Let be . . .
Let God . . .

Be rooted and grounded in Love,
for Love is the Ground of our being . . .
Be drawn through Love's narrow gate,
For Love is the Goal of our becoming . . .

It takes courage to look steadily at ourselves and still to love
  ourselves . . .

Deep down in the bowels of everyone there lives a horrible
unclean larva. Lean over and say to this larva, I love you,
and it will sprout wings and become a butterfly . . .   [36]

We are on this earth that we may learn to *bear* the *beams* of
love . . .   [37]

Only so can our love for others be a burning gentleness . . .
                                                          [38]

If you have no love for your own lasting interest, if you hate
your own soul (and show it by loving evil), how can you love
the very being, the deepest interests, of another? . . .   [39]

Do not despair, never give up hope for yourself or for one
another. Bitter enemies and lost friends can become friends
again. Love that has grown cold can kindle and burst into
flame . . .   [40]

   Rejoice in the impossibilities,
   the incompletions,
   from within which alone the future is shaped and given
      meaning.
   Listen to the whisper of the thunder on a distant
      shore . . .

                        ❖

WE depend on the earth for three things –
   for sex – and we are ill at ease;
   for food – and we are anxious;
   for survival – and we dread death . . .

Jesus of Nazareth:
   the God of desire fills his being;
   the will of God is done out of desire;
   my *food* is to do the will of God who sent me . . .

Jesus of Nazareth: totally at one with God –
   and so at ease with sexuality,
      emotionally open to both women and men;
   not at all anxious about food;
   accepting death as his destiny . . .

Jesus of Nazareth:
   Let him awaken in us limitless desire for bliss . . .
   Let him focus and crystallise that desire . . .
   Let him take that desire to the point of his death . . .
   Let us be totally nothing with him . . .
   Let us be filled with the Spirit of God
      who brings life and joy out of death . . .   [41]

❖

ABBA, I abandon myself into your hands . . .
In your love for me do as you will . . .
Whatever that may prove to be I am thankful . . .
I am ready for all, I accept all . . .
Let only your will be done in me,
as in all your creatures,
and I will ask nothing else . . .
Into your hands I commend my whole being . . .
I give you my self with the love of my heart . . .
For I love you, my God, and so I need to give . . .
to surrender myself into your hands . . .
with a trust beyond measure . . .
For you are my faithful Creator . . .
Abba . . .
Friend . . .   [42]

❖

COVENANT of God and with God:

I Who Am and Who Shall Be
have chosen to share my life with you, N.
By my own name and nature,
I continually affirm, renew, and deepen
my promise to love you for ever,
to honour you as my dwelling place,
and to be loyal to you
and full of faith in you,
our life-day long.
Amen. So be it.

❖

I, N, of my own free will,
have chosen to share my life with you,
Yahweh my God.
And I affirm, renew, and deepen
my promise to love you for ever,
to honour you as the Great Spirit within me,
and the Great Presence beyond me,
and the Great Future before me,
shown to me in Yeshua ben Yosef of Nazareth,
and to be loyal to you
and full of faith in you,
our life-day long.
Amen. So be it.

❖

Covenant of Friendship:

In the Mystery of Divine Love,
you have been given to me, N,
and in my own free will and destiny,
I embrace you,
choosing and being chosen
to share with you my being and becoming.
And with and in that Love,
I promise to be for you
and for your well-being for ever,
to honour you as a dwelling place of God,
and to be loyal to you
and full of faith in you,
our life-day long.

✠

O God of the living,
in whose embrace all creatures live,
in whatever world or condition they may be,
I pray for those whose names and needs
    and dwelling place are known to you . . .
giving you thanks for my memories of them.
In you, O God, I love them.
May this my prayer minister
    to their growing and their peace;
in and through Jesus Christ,
    who broke the barrier of death
    and lives for evermore.   [43]

✠

THIS is the place of prayer,
Here, where the inward-pointing nails
converge.
The ever-narrowing gate
intersection
when the world of time and space
yields up its measured form.

Here in the needle's eye
Dark upon dark.
The aching, echoing void
of the hollowed heart
suspended
at the point of change.

Unknowing
(and that is the agony)
bearing the unknown
to the mystery
at the place of prayer.   [44]

❖

WE need a way of seeing in the dark . . .   [45]

❖

THERE is in God, some say,
  a deep but dazzling darkness . . .   [46]

❖

METHINKS there is in God
  a well of laughter very deep . . .   [47]

❖

NOTES
AND ACKNOWLEDGMENTS

PRAYERS OF INTRODUCTION AND OF RECOGNITION, AND PSALMS

In the prayers of recognition, confession is set in the context of gratitude and affirmation of acceptance and forgiveness, the latter receiving more emphasis than usual, and perhaps to be bathed in silence. The Psalms are paraphrases, and some of the wording has been derived from various English translations, ancient and modern.

Sunday: Psalm 103 (with a *New Testament* addition)
Monday: Psalms 134; 4; 23
Tuesday: Psalms 121; 16.7–11; 31.1–5
Wednesday: Psalm 139.1–18
Thursday: Psalms 46; 91.1–5, 11, 14–16
Friday: Psalms 130; 126
Saturday: Psalms 42; 43

READINGS

The readings are scriptural. Those for Days 1–8 are paraphrases of the Beatitudes. That for Day 30 is a paraphrase of 1 Cor.13. The reading for Christmas is John 1.14 with comment, and that for the Departed is based on the *Alternative Service Book*.

HYMNS

The hymns are mostly ancient evening hymns somewhat adapted. That for Saturday is new, and can be sung to the tune of *The Ash Grove*.

PRAYERS

The extended paraphrase of the Lord's Prayer is by the compiler. Of the prayers for each day of the month, that for Day 11 is based on a prayer by George Appleton in *One Man's Prayers* and owes much to the Buddhist tradition.

1. Dag Hammarskjöld
2. Taizé Community
3. Taizé Community
4. ?
5. Book of Common Prayer
6. Victor Gollancz
7. Compiler, after the Jesus Prayer
8. Compiler
9. Week of Prayer for World Peace
10. Week of Prayer for World Peace
11. After George Appleton
12. Psalm 78.72 Authorised Version
13. A Liberation Prayer Book
14. Elizabeth Basset
15. B.C.P. adapted
16. B.C.P. adapted
17. Richard of Chichester
18. B.C.P. adapted
19. B.C.P. adapted
20. B.C.P. adapted
21. B.C.P. adapted
22. Bahai adapted
23. Sid Hedges
24. Kabir
25. Trevor Huddleston
26. Let My People Go, ed. M. Evans
27. Let My People Go
28. Alan Paton
29. B.C.P. adapted
30. B.C.P. adapted
31. Alan Paton

CAIRNS FOR A JOURNEY

1. Lord Dunsanay
2. John Buchan
3. Carl Jung (quote)
4. Alan Jones
5. George Appleton (adapted)
6. Dag Hammarskjöld
7. Max Warren
8. Dag Hammarskjöld
9. W.H. Auden
10. David Jones
11. World Council of Churches
12. Rainer Maria Rilke (adapted)
13. Monica Furlong
14. Sebastian Moore
15. Friedrich Nietzsche
16. Rainer Maria Rilke
17. Charles Williams
18. R.S. Shannon
19. Léon Bloy
20. J.S. Collis
21. W.H. Auden
22. Stevie Smith
23. O.V. de L. Milosz
24. Angelus Silesius (quote)
25. William Blake (quote)
26. Julian of Norwich (adapted)
27. Michelangelo
28. G.M. Hopkins
29. L. Clarke & J. Nichols
30. Merle Miller (adapted)
31. Sebastian Moore (adapted)
32. Andrew Elphinstone
33. W.H. Auden
34. Philip Larkin
35. Rainer Maria Rilke
36. Nikos Kazantzakis
37. William Blake
38. Pierre Teilhard de Chardin
39. Aelred of Rievaulx
40. Søren Kierkegaard
41. Sebastian Moore (adapted)
42. Charles de Foucauld (adapted)
43. J.V. Taylor (adapted)
44. May Crowther
45. Peter Shaffer
46. Henry Vaughan
47. ?